About the Marine Sanctuaries Conservation Series

The National Oceanic and Atmospheric Administration administers the National Marine Sanctuary Program. Its mission is to identify, designate, protect and manage the ecological, recreational, research, educational, historical, and aesthetic resources and qualities of nationally significant coastal and marine areas. The existing marine sanctuaries differ widely in their natural and historical resources and include nearshore and open ocean areas ranging in size from less than one to over 5,000 square miles. Protected habitats include rocky coasts, kelp forests, coral reefs, sea grass beds, estuarine habitats, hard and soft bottom habitats, segments of whale migration routes, and shipwrecks.

Because of considerable differences in settings, resources, and threats, each marine sanctuary has a tailored management plan. Conservation, education, research, monitoring and enforcement programs vary accordingly. The integration of these programs is fundamental to marine protected area management. The Marine Sanctuaries Conservation Series reflects and supports this integration by providing a forum for publication and discussion of the complex issues currently facing the National Marine Sanctuary Program. Topics of published reports vary substantially and may include descriptions of educational programs, discussions on resource management issues, and results of scientific research and monitoring projects. The series facilitates integration of natural sciences, socioeconomic and cultural sciences, education, and policy development to accomplish the diverse needs of NOAA's resource protection mandate.

M/V *JACQUELYN L*
Coral Reef Restoration Monitoring Report
Monitoring Events 2004-2005
Florida Keys National Marine Sanctuary
Monroe County, Florida

Erik C. Franklin
J. Harold Hudson
Jeff Anderson
Joe Schittone

Florida Keys National Marine Sanctuary
National Marine Sanctuaries Program, National Ocean Service
National Oceanic and Atmospheric Administration

U.S. Department of Commerce
Carlos M. Gutierrez, Secretary

National Oceanic and Atmospheric Administration
VADM Conrad C. Lautenbacher, Jr. (USN-ret.)
Under Secretary of Commerce for Oceans and Atmosphere

National Ocean Service
John H. Dunnigan, Assistant Administrator

Silver Spring, Maryland
October 2006

National Marine Sanctuary Program
Daniel J. Basta, Director

DISCLAIMER

The mention of trade names or commercial products does not constitute endorsement or recommendation for use.

REPORT AVAILABILITY

Electronic copies of this report may be downloaded from the National Marine Sanctuaries Program web site at http://www.sanctuaries.noaa.gov/. Hard copies may be available from the following address:

National Oceanic and Atmospheric Administration
National Marine Sanctuary Program
SSMC4, N/ORM62
1305 East-West Highway
Silver Spring, MD 20910

COVER

Acropora palmata colonies on Western Sambo Reef near the M/V *Jacquelyn L* restoration site, Florida Keys National Marine Sanctuary. Photo credit: Jeff Anderson.

SUGGESTED CITATION

Franklin, E.C., Hudson, J.H., Anderson, J., Schittone, J. 2006. M/V *Jacquelyn L* Coral Reef Restoration Monitoring Report, Monitoring Events 2004-2005. Florida Keys National Marine Sanctuary Monroe County, Florida. Marine Sanctuaries Conservation Series NMSP-06-09. U.S. Department of Commerce, National Oceanic and Atmospheric Administration, National Marine Sanctuary Program, Silver Spring, MD. 21 pp.

CONTACT

Joe Schittone, corresponding author, at: Joe.Schittone@noaa.gov

ABSTRACT

This document presents the results of the monitoring of a repaired coral reef injured by the M/V *Jacquelyn L* vessel grounding incident of July 7, 1991. This grounding occurred in Florida state waters within the boundaries of the Florida Keys National Marine Sanctuary (FKNMS). The National Oceanic and Atmospheric Administration (NOAA) and the Board of Trustees of the Internal Improvement Trust Fund of the State of Florida, ("State of Florida" or "state") are the co-trustees for the natural resources within the FKNMS and, thus, are responsible for mediating the restoration of the damaged marine resources and monitoring the outcome of the restoration actions. The restoration monitoring program tracks patterns of biological recovery, determines the success of restoration measures, and assesses the resiliency to environmental and anthropogenic disturbances of the site over time.

The monitoring program at the *Jacquelyn L* site was to have included an assessment of the structural stability of installed restoration modules and biological condition of reattached corals performed on the following schedule: immediately (i.e., baseline), 1, 3, and 6 years after restoration and following a catastrophic event. Restoration of this site was completed on July 20, 2000. Due to unavoidable delays in the settlement of the case, the "baseline" monitoring event for this site occurred in July 2004. The catastrophic monitoring event occurred on August 31, 2004, some 2 ½ weeks after the passage of Hurricane Charley which passed nearby, almost directly over the Dry Tortugas. In September 2005, the year one monitoring event occurred shortly after the passage of Hurricane Katrina, some 70 km to the NW. This report presents the results of all three monitoring events.

KEY WORDS

Florida Keys National Marine Sanctuary, coral, grounding, restoration, monitoring, Hurricane Charley, Hurricane Katrina, *Acropora palmata*

TABLE OF CONTENTS

LIST OF FIGURES AND TABLES

ACKNOWLEDGEMENTS

The National Oceanic and Atmospheric Administration (NOAA) and the Board of Trustees of the Internal Improvement Trust Fund of the State of Florida, ("State of Florida" or "state") are the co-trustees for the natural resources within the FKNMS and, thus, are responsible for mediating the restoration of the damaged marine resources and monitoring the outcome of the restoration actions. The authors would like to express their appreciation to all Florida Department of Environmental Protection employees who participated in the initial response, damage assessment, restoration, and case settlement associated with this vessel grounding.

INTRODUCTION

This document presents the results of baseline monitoring of a repaired coral reef injured by the M/V *Jacquelyn L* vessel grounding incident of July 7, 1991. This grounding occurred in Florida state waters within the boundaries of the Florida Keys National Marine Sanctuary (FKNMS). The National Oceanic and Atmospheric Administration (NOAA) and the Board of Trustees of the Internal Improvement Trust Fund of the State of Florida, ("State of Florida" or "state") are the co-trustees for the natural resources within the FKNMS and, thus, are responsible for mediating the restoration of the damaged marine resources and monitoring the outcome of the restoration actions. The restoration monitoring program tracks patterns of biological recovery, determines the success of restoration measures, and assesses the resiliency to environmental and anthropogenic disturbances of the site over time. To evaluate restoration success, reference habitats adjacent to the restoration site are concurrently monitored to compare the condition of restored reef areas with "natural" coral reef areas unimpacted by the vessel grounding.

The monitoring program at the *Jacquelyn L* site included an assessment of the structural stability of installed restoration modules and biological condition of reattached corals, which was to have performed on the following schedule: immediately (i.e., baseline), 1, 3, and 6 years after restoration and following a catastrophic event (Table 1). Restoration of this site was completed on July 20, 2000. Due to unavoidable delays in the settlement of the case, the "baseline" monitoring event for this site occurred in 2004. Hurricane Charley (August 2004) passed almost directly over the Dry Tortugas triggered the post-catastrophic monitoring event, which occurred on August 31, 2004. The year one monitoring event was to have taken place in the summer of 2005. In the early summer of that year, Hurricanes Dennis and Katrina, the later of which passed the site about 60 km to the NW, transpired before a monitoring effort at the site could be mounted. However, the site was visited shortly after the passage of Hurricane Katrina, in mid-September 2005. At that time the site was found to be nearly obliterated, with essentially no coral colonies, or even fragments of same, remaining. Since there was nothing left to monitor, no quantitative data from the event was collected. Needless to say, the scheduled Year Three and Year Six monitoring events will no longer take place.

Table 1. Event timeline for the M/V *Jacquelyn L* grounding site restoration.

Event	Date
Vessel Grounding	July 7, 1991
Assessment: Initial	July 9, 1991
Restoration: Uprighted overturned corals	July 11, 1991
Restoration	June 20-July 20, 2000
Baseline Monitoring	*July 13-14, 2004*
Post-catastrophic Monitoring	August 31, 2004
Year One Monitoring	September 13,2005

Damage Assessment

[Note: The information in this section was adapted from the Discussion section of the *Jacquelyn L* Vessel Grounding Assessment prepared by J. Harold Hudson]

The *Jacquelyn L*, a 16.5 m motor vessel, struck and damaged the shallow reef crest at Western Sambo reef, located south of Boca Chica Key on July 7, 1991 (Figure 1). The predominant coral species observed within the injured area was the elkhorn coral *Acropora palmata* (Lamarck, 1816). Other coral species present included mustard hill coral (*Porites astreoides*), lettuce coral (*Agaricia agaricites*), brain coral (*Diploria strigosa*), fire coral (*Millepora complanata*), golfball coral (*Favia fragum*) and starlet coral (*Siderastrea siderea*). Other living components of the injured area included crustaceans, macroalgae, sponges, echinoderms, mollusks, octocorals and fish.

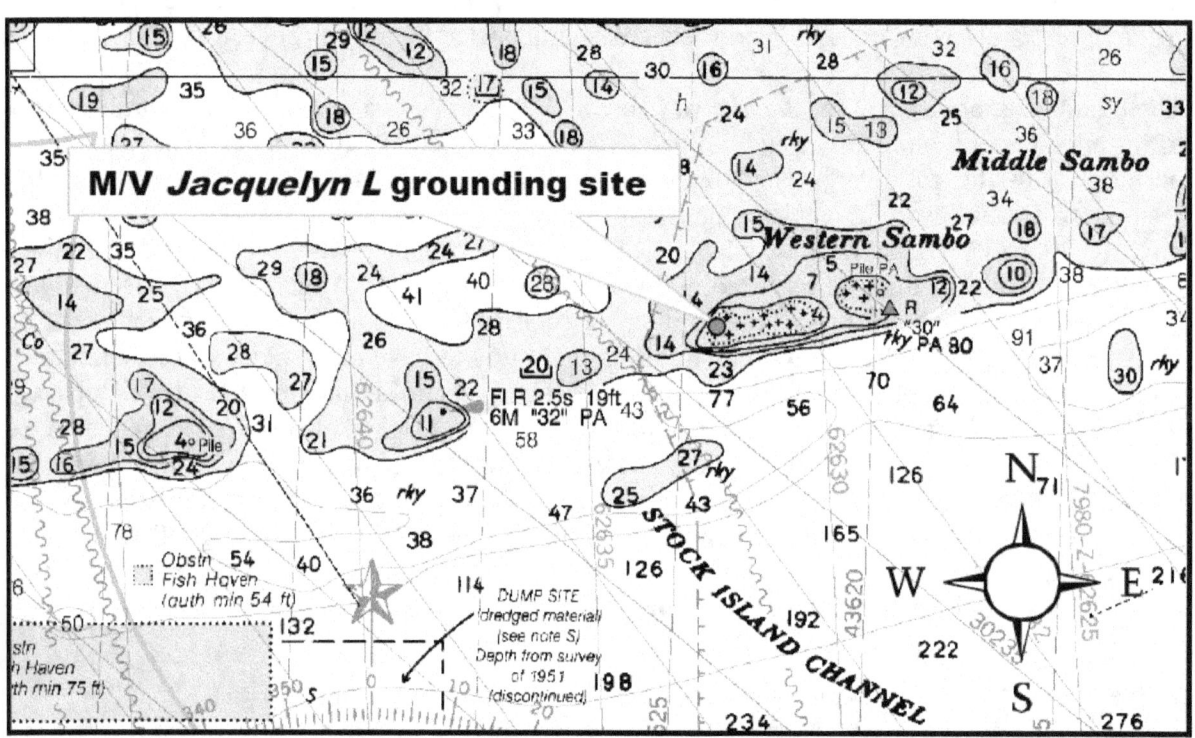

Figure 1. Approximate location (shown on NOAA Chart 11442) that the M/V *Jacquelyn L* ran aground on the reef crest of Western Sambo Reef on July 7, 1991.

The most prominent feature of the injury site consisted of a wide grounding track plowed through *Acropora palmata* thickets. The grounding track was 107.5 m long on a heading of 69°. During removal, the vessel was extracted along a heading of 264° (Figure 2). The grounding damaged 23 sites along the inbound path (Table 2). The area of damaged reef framework from the inbound path, resting place, and outbound path was 73 m². The area of injured corals was 123.8125 m², predominately the *Acropora palmata*. Finally, the total injury area of reef framework and corals was 196.81 m²).

2

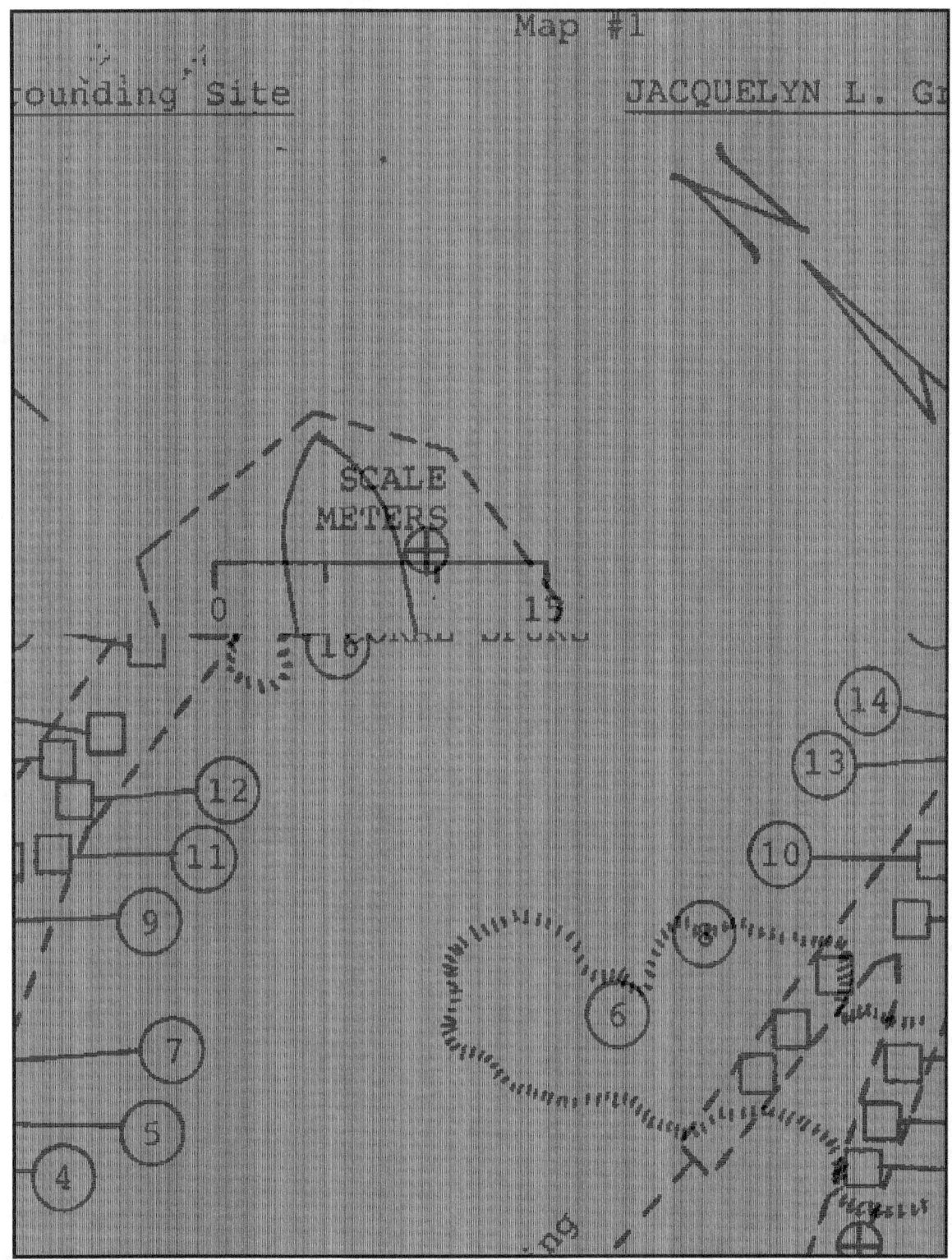

Figure 2. Diagram of the M/V *Jacquelyn L* grounding track and damaged areas of Western Sambo Reef.

Table 2. Summary of live coral damage along the grounding track of the *Jacquelyn L* (see Figure 2. for location of damage sites; from Hudson 1991).

Site #	Coral Species	Damage (Total/Partial)	Coral Cover (%)	Area (m^2)
1	*Millepora complanata*	Total	100 %	.2500
2	*Acropora palmata*	Total	100 %	.2500
3	*A. palmata*	Total	100 %	1.0000
4	*A. palmata*	Total	100 %	.5000
5	*A. palmata*	Partial	100 %	.5000
6	*A. palmata*	Total	100 %	2.0000
7	*A. palmata*	Total	100 %	1.0000
8	*A. palmata*	Total	100 %	1.0000
9	*A. palmata*	Total	100 %	.2500
10	*A. palmata*	Total	100 %	.2500
11	*A. palmata*	Total	100 %	.2500
12	*A. palmata*	Total	100 %	.2500
13	*Diploria strigosa*	Total	100 %	.1250
14-A	*A. palmata*	Total	100 %	2.0000
14-B	*Gorgonia ventalina*	Total	100 %	.1250
15	*A. palmata*	Total	100 %	1.5000
16	*Siderastrea siderea*	Total	100 %	.7500
17	*A. palmata*	Total	100 %	3.0000
18-A	*A. palmata*	Total	100 %	13.7500
18-B	*M. complanata*	Total	100 %	1.0000
19	*A. palmata*	Total	100 %	14.2000
20-A	*A. palmata*	Total	100 %	79.8000
20-B	*Porites astreoides*	Total	100 %	.0625
			Total	**123.8215**

Coral Reef Restoration

The objectives of the M/V *Jacquelyn L* site restoration were to 1) salvage and reattach dislodged *Acropora palmata* fragments and 2) transplant *Acropora palmata* colonies from outside the grounding site to the final resting place of the vessel (see Damage Site #20 in Figure 2). To accomplish these objectives, seventy-seven *Acropora palmata* colonies and five "coral rosettes" of *A. palmata* were transplanted and reattached to the vessel's resting place (Figure 3). Coral colony size was not recorded during restoration. Coral rosettes were colonies affixed to concrete pavers which were cemented to the substrate. The remainder of the colonies were affixed to the substrate with Portland Type II cement grout. Locations for colony reattachment were determined haphazardly by FKNMS staff during the restoration efforts.

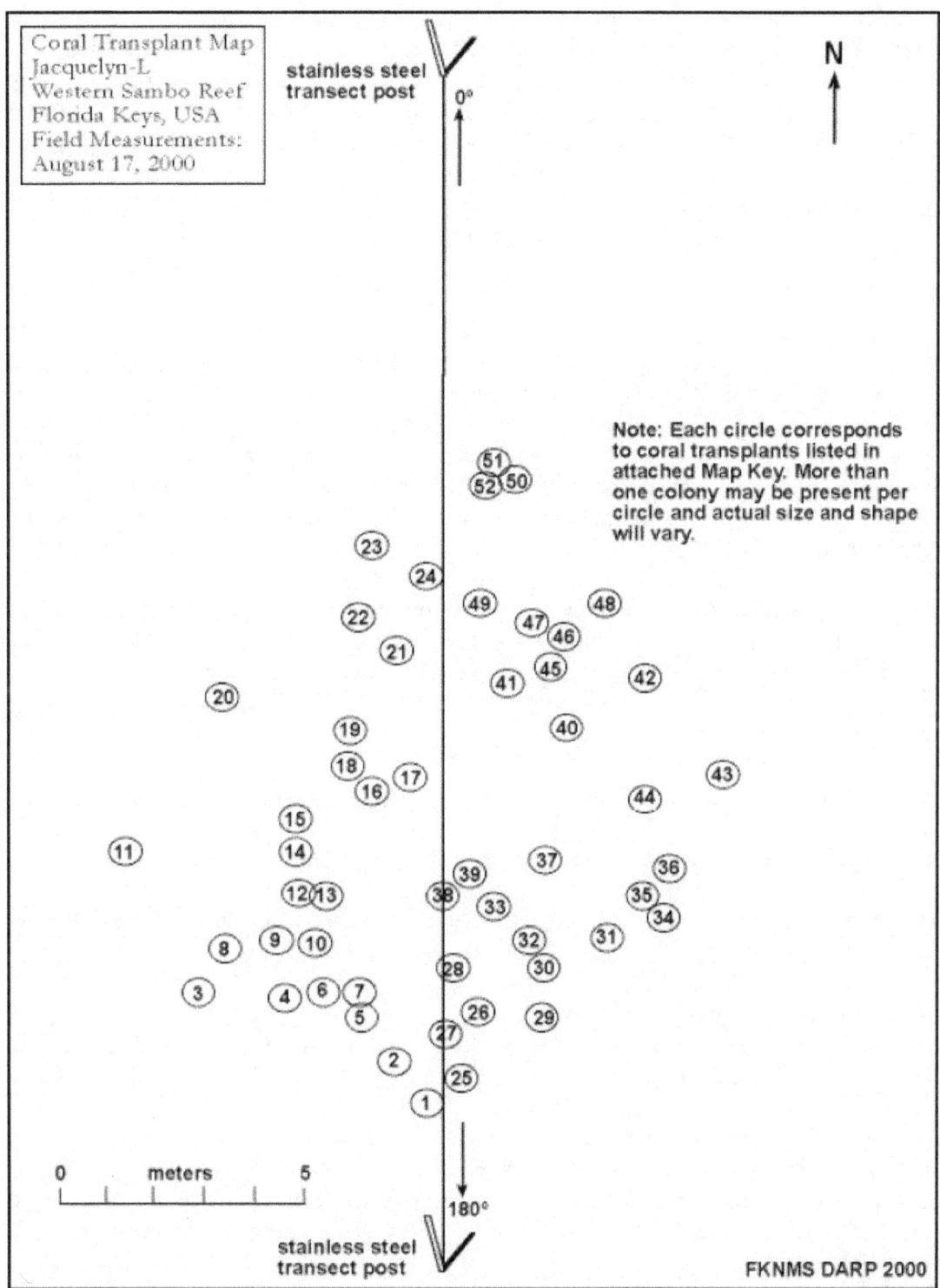

Figure 3. Location of reattached and transplanted *Acropora palmata* colonies at the *Jacquelyn L* grounding site.

Project oversight was provided by Harold Hudson, FKNMS, with the restoration performed by FKNMS and NOAA staff. Field operations during the habitat restoration were conducted using a 9-m (30-ft) Gulfstream® vessel with sufficient deck space to allow transport of reef replacement modules and to accommodate SCUBA and construction equipment. A 6.4-m (21-ft) Carolina Skiff® with minimal draft was used during specialized vessel operations along the impact track. On-board navigation during transit to and from the project site was achieved using a Garmin differential global positioning system (DGPS).

Restoration Monitoring

The purpose of the coral restoration monitoring program is to evaluate the success of trustee actions in achieving restoration goals and to determine if remedial measures are needed. For a grounding site such as the M/V *Jacquelyn L*, the evaluation of restoration efforts involves the identification of appropriate success criteria and the design and implementation of a sampling and analysis plan. A list of success criteria measures for structural and functional aspects of coral reef restoration as well as a framework for monitoring activities is identified by NOAA (Thayer et al. 2003).

The guiding hypotheses for the evaluation of the "restoration" site reflects the efficacy of the restoration techniques and the condition of the site relative to reference habitats. The monitoring program addresses if the chosen restoration methods are effective and when the site could be considered restored. The structural integrity of the restoration site is evaluated with the following questions:

1. Are the attachments to the substrate of the reattached or transplanted *Acropora palmata* colonies stable?
2. Is there any visible physical damage to the reattached coral colonies?

In addition, the biological condition of the restoration site was evaluated with the following questions:

1. Is there live coral tissue on the colonies?
2. Is there a difference in coral cover between the grounding site (i.e., both the restored and unrestored areas) and the reference area?

The monitoring program was designed to detect significant changes in coral cover or damage to restoration components (structural enhancements, coral transplants, etc.) as a result of external events, such as major storms or vandalism, and in comparison to the surrounding habitat. In addition, the monitoring assessed the effectiveness of the restoration based upon technical evaluation of appropriate parameters.

METHODOLOGY

Field Methods

On July 13-14, 2004, the *Jacquelyn L* restoration site was monitored using SCUBA from a small vessel (6.4 m). Use of the restoration site map (Figure 3) to identify individual reattached colonies was not possible because the stake at the southern end of the restoration transect was missing. Twenty-seven reattached *Acropora palmata* colonies were either located visually (as in the case of the rosettes) or by chipping at the colony base with a geological hammer to search for a cement attachment. Numbered identification tags (e.g., "J01" to "J27") were attached to the base of the colonies with large zip-ties (see APPENDIX 1 for photos). Tactile and visual stability assessments were performed by attempting to displace twenty-five of the reattached coral colonies. In addition, the height, width, length, and percent live tissue of each of these colonies were recorded following the method of Rogers et al. (2004). To determine the biological condition of the site, *in situ* observations, digital images, and digital videos were recorded from 1 m^2 quadrats surveyed in the restoration area and the reference area. Due to the age of the grounding site, the boundary of the damaged, unrestored area was unidentifiable. The reference area was adjacent to the northwest side of the grounding path and similar in size and shape to the damaged area (i.e., approximately 197 m^2). Within the reference area, twenty 1 m^2 cells were randomly chosen from a digital grid of uniquely identified 1 m^2 cells overlain on the grounding site map. In the field, transect lines were used from landmarks to determine cell locations as best as possible. Quadrats were deployed to these cells and visually surveyed for biological variables of interest. Quadrats were centered over the areas occupied by the located transplanted colonies. Within each quadrat, the percent coral cover and the presence of coral disease, coral bleaching, and damselfish were recorded. In addition, the number of sea urchins, corallivorous snails, and lobsters were also recorded in each quadrat. Planar digital photographs of quadrats were recorded when depth allowed, while oblique digital photographs were taken of each tagged *A. palmata* colony in the restored area. Underwater digital images were collected with an Olympus C-5050 digital camera in a Light & Motion Tetra 5050 underwater housing and digital videos were collected with a Sony DCR-DVD200 video camera in an Amphibico QuickView DVD underwater housing.

On August 31, 2004, the post-catastrophic monitoring event (post Hurricane Charley) took place. The methodology was as related above. In mid-September 2005, what was to have been the Year One monitoring event occurred. However, as related above, this was shortly after the passage of Hurricanes Dennis and Katrina, both relatively near to the restoration site. One or the other, or a combination of both storms nearly obliterated the site, leaving no intact coral colonies, almost no standing coral, and very few coral fragments. Therefore, no quantitative data was collected, and it would no longer be appropriate to continue to monitor this site.

Photo Analysis

Digital images were edited with Adobe Photoshop version 7 (Adobe 2002). Image edits included color hue changes to make water look more blue, brightness changes to compensate for original exposure, and sharpness changes to enhance images not in focus. Planar images of quadrats were corrected using the Panorama Tools plug-in for Photoshop to correct for barrel distortion of the extreme wide angle image making it as close to square as possible. Finally, excess image information outside the quadrat boundary was cropped.

Data Analysis

Data analysis and visualization were performed on a Dell PC with Statistica version 6 (StatSoft 2003) and Microsoft® Excel 2002 software. Basic descriptive statistics were generated for samples collected among the restoration and reference areas.

RESULTS

BASELINE MONITORING EVENT

Structural Integrity

The baseline monitoring occurred in July 2004, at which time the stability of twenty five reattached/transplanted *Acropora palmata* colonies were found to be visually and tactically sound (Table 3). The colonies were found in place with a stable attachment to the substrate and no visible cracks in the cement grout surface. There was no noticeable physical damage to the reattached coral fragments although there were signs of past tissue loss (see photos in APPENDIX 1).

Table 3. Baseline monitoring event—observed physical and biological characteristics of reattached coral colonies at *Jacquelyn L* site.

A. palmata colony (#)	Stable Attachment (Yes/No)	Physical Damage (Yes/No)	Coral Tissue (%)	Max. Length (cm)	Max. Width (cm)	Max. Height (cm)
1	Yes	No	100	45	40	32
2	Yes	No	100	39	29	29
3	Yes	No	100	32	23	22
4	Yes	No	20	7	4	9
5	Yes	No	35	9	6	14
6	Yes	No	25	36	28	33
7	Yes	No	95	36	31	21
8	Yes	No	80	56	47	29
9	Yes	No	85	21	19	15
10	Yes	No	100	12	10	11
11	Yes	No	95	98	64	38
12	Yes	No	75	56	42	37
13	Yes	No	80	111	89	47
14	Yes	No	95	56	43	27
15	Yes	No	65	54	38	30
16	Yes	No	35	61	31	39
17	Yes	No	65	49	46	36
18	Yes	No	100	13	9	13
19	Yes	No	90	92	76	35
20	Yes	No	95	72	58	34
21	Yes	No	99	44	38	28
22	Yes	No	90	68	45	36
23	Yes	No	95	84	54	38
24	Yes	No	75	44	29	27
25	Yes	No	95	62	34	42

Biological Condition

The *Jacquelyn L* restoration site contained a matrix of solitary live *Acropora palmata* colonies, live *A. palmata* thickets, dead *A. palmata* skeletons, and reef rubble. Coral species observed within quadrats included *Acropora palmata*, *Favia fragum*, *Millepora alcicornis*, and *Porites astreoides*. *Acropora palmata* was the dominant coral species and represented 98% of the reported coral cover. Reflecting the habitat matrix of the reef flat, samples of coral cover within areas were heterogeneous; cover ranged from 4% to 49% in the restored area and from 0% to 58% in the reference area. Mean coral cover was 29% in the restored area and 19% in the reference area (Figure 4).

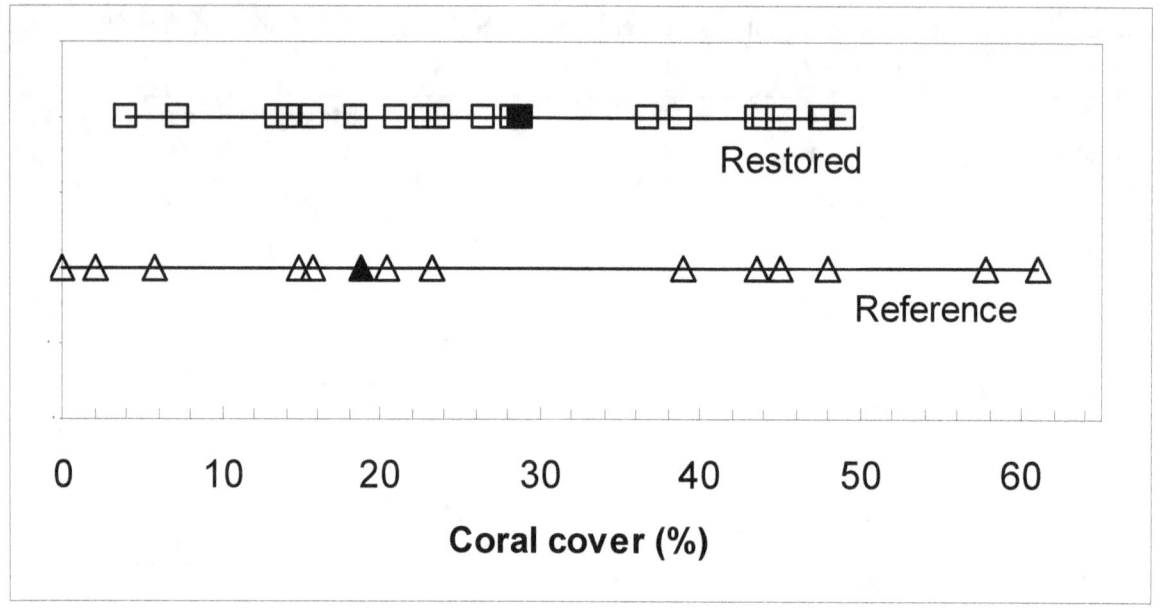

Figure 4. Baseline monitoring event—Sample observations with means (solid, dark symbols) of coral cover (%) recorded from the restored area and the reference area of the *Jacquelyn L* grounding site (n=20 for each). [Note: In the reference area, %=0 for seven of the observations.]

The density of sea urchins was found to be greater in the restored area. In the restored area, sea urchin density was 0.1 urchins m^{-2}, composed entirely of long-spined sea urchin (*Diadema antillarum*). In the reference area, only slate pencil sea urchins (*Eucidaris tribuloides*) were observed, with a density of 0.05 urchins m^{-2} (Figure 5). There were no lobsters or corallivorous snails (*Coralliophila* sp.) observed in any quadrats.

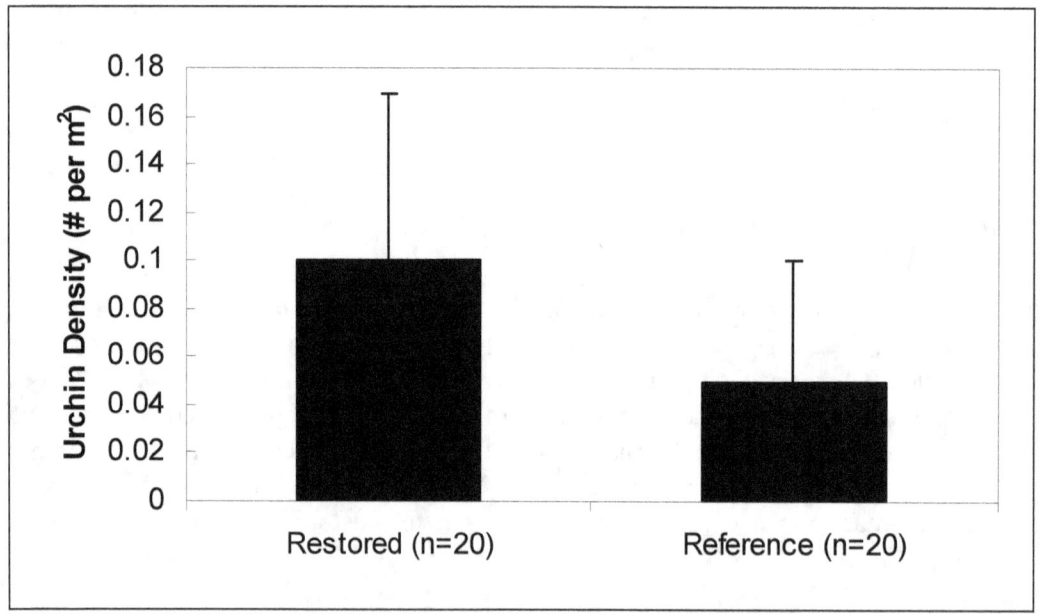

Figure 5. Baseline monitoring event—urchin density at restored and reference sites.

The presence of damselfish and diseased or bleached corals were recorded among the two areas. Damselfish were observed among 25% of quadrats in the reference habitat while only present in 10% of the restored area. White pox was observed on one colony, reattached *Acropora palmata* colony #4. Coral "paling" was observed on several colonies. White band disease was not observed in either of the areas.

POST-CATASTROPHIC MONITORING EVENT

Structural Integrity

The majority of reattached/transplanted *Acropora palmata* colonies withstood the hurricane event. The bases of most colonies remained affixed to the substrate. However, as can be expected in a storm event, there was noticeable physical damage to some reattached coral colonies. The tips of some fragments appeared to have been recently broken and some tagged colonies were toppled (see photos in APPENDIX 2). At this monitoring event, 3 of the 27 identification tags (see above, METHODOLOGY—*Field Methods*) and the colonies to which they were affixed, could no longer be located.

Biological Condition

At this monitoring event coral cover of the restored area declined from the 29% it had been one month before Hurricane Charley, to 20.5% (Figure 6). It should be noted that the majority of this coverage decline was due to the three missing colonies that had comprised part of the sampled area. In other words, for the coral colonies that remained affixed, although tissue damage and skeletal fragmentation were observed, the majority of colonies suffered either no or relatively minor injuries. Meanwhile, the reference area evidenced essentially no change from the baseline pre-Hurricane Charley monitoring event (July) to the immediately post-hurricane monitoring (August), even seeming to increase by 0.9% (though this is well within the standard error of the means of the sampling distribution; Figure 6).

YEAR ONE MONITORING EVENT

As previously related, the Year One monitoring event was conducted on September 13, 2005. This was after the near passage of Hurricane Dennis in July, and Hurricane Katrina in August. The status of the site after the passage of one or the other (or possibly the combination of both) of these later hurricanes presented a much bleaker picture than was evidenced after Hurricane Charley the previous year. [Note: those familiar with the area will remember that Hurricanes Rita and Wilma also struck the vicinity in 2005; however, both these storms occurred after the Year One monitoring event in September.]

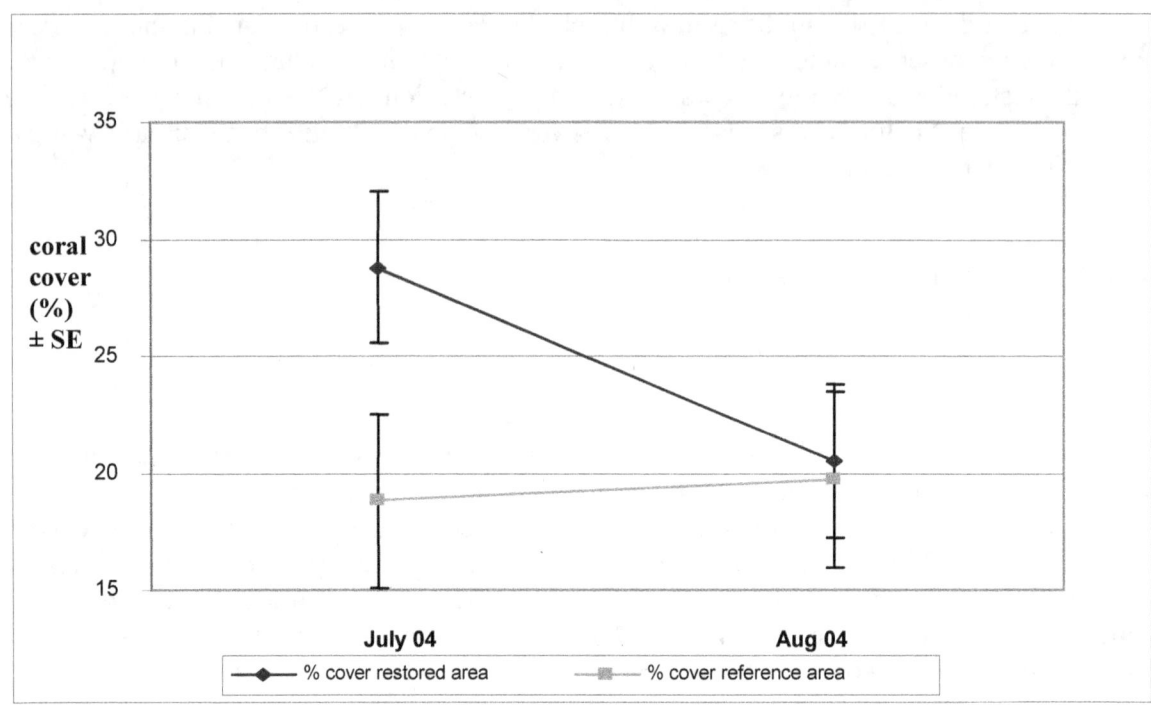

Figure 6. Comparison of Pre (July)- and Post (Aug.)-hurricane Charley % coral cover of restored and reference areas (n=20 for all data points).

After the passage of hurricanes Dennis and Katrina, the field monitoring team could barely locate the restoration site. Five of the 24 colonies which remained after Hurricane Charley of the previous year were identified. Those colonies remaining, while showing signs of positive tissue growth prior to the storms (see photos of Colony #7 in APPENDIX 3), suffered loss of both skeletal and tissue elements (see photos in APPENDIX 3). Destruction of the restored area can be directly traced to instability of the underlying substrate. Close inspection of the site revealed that instead of a well-cemented reef framework, the reef underpinning there was composed of loose *Acropora palmata* debris held in place by tightly-packed sediment. Washout of the stabilizing sediment by hurricane-driven waves allowed the massive sections of *A. palmata* debris that the transplants were cemented on to be swept away.

SUMMARY

Baseline monitoring suggested that the reattachment of coral colonies with Portland cement grout was an effective restoration method for *Acropora palmata* thickets damaged at Western Sambo reef by the *Jacquelyn L.* Structural stability of the reattached colonies was generally excellent with no colonies showing physical damage (Table 3). Coral cover at the repaired grounding site was higher than the reference area (Figure 4). However, the close passage of 3 powerful hurricanes over the course of the next two years alters this assessment. The restoration area has essentially been obliterated, and any further monitoring is not warranted.

Comparison to the monitoring report regarding the M/V *Connected* site (q.v., in the Sanctuaries' "Conservation Series"), which lies almost immediately adjacent to the *Jacquelyn L* site, should prove informative. Although the groundings at the two sites were separated by a decade, the restorations took place only a year apart (*Jacquelyn L* in July 2000; *Connected* in July 2001). Thus the sites had 3 & 4 years respectively to establish themselves before the passage of Hurricane Charley in 2004, and 4 & 5 years before Hurricanes Dennis and Katrina in 2005 (with the *Jacquelyn L* site having the extra year). The much greater success enjoyed by the *Connected* restoration, in both years, provides much in the way of valuable information and "lessons learned" to the Damage Assessment & Restoration Team of the National Marine Sanctuary Program.

LITERATURE CITED

Adobe, Inc. 2002. Photoshop (image processing software), version 7. www.adobe.com.

Hudson, J. H. 1991. *Jacquelyn L* vessel grounding assessment report. Confidential report prepared for NOAA General Counsel and FDEP Office of General Counsel. 3 pp. plus figures.

Rogers C, Loomis C, Devine B. 2004. A new protocol for surveying elkhorn and staghorn coral. Reef Encounter 31:49-51.

StatSoft, Inc. 2003. STATISTICA (data analysis software system), version 6. www.statsoft.com.

Thayer, G. W. , T. A. McTigue, R. J. Bellmer, F. M. Burrows, D. H. Merkey, A. D. Nickens, S.J. Lozano, P. F. Gayaldo, P. J. Polmateer, and P. T. Pinit. 2003. Science-based restoration monitoring of coastal habitats, volume one: A framework for monitoring plans under the Estuaries and Clean Waters Act of 2000 (Public Law 160-457). NOAA Coastal Ocean Program Decision Analysis Series No.23, Volume 1. NOAA National Centers for Coastal Ocean Science, Silver Spring, MD. 35 pp. plus appendices.

Zar, J. H. 1984. Biostatistical analysis. 2nd edition. Englewood Cliffs, New Jersey: Prentice-Hall International.

APPENDIX 1

Photographs of reattached/transplanted coral colonies at the M/V *Jacquelyn L* grounding site taken on July 14, 2004.

Colony #13

Colony #14

Colony #15

Colony #16

Colony #17

Colony #18

Colony #25

Colony #26

Colony #27

Photographs of toppled, tagged coral colonies at the M/V *Jacquelyn L* grounding site taken on August 31, 2004.

APPENDIX 3

Photographs of reattached/transplanted coral colonies and restoration area at the M/V *Jacquelyn L* grounding site taken on September 13, 2005.

NMSP CONSERVATION SERIES PUBLICATIONS

To date, the following reports have been published in the Marine Sanctuaries Conservation Series. All publications are available on the National Marine Sanctuary Program website (http://www.sanctuaries.noaa.gov/).

M/V *WAVE WALKER* Coral Reef Restoration Baseline Monitoring Report - 2004 Florida Keys National Marine Sanctuary Monroe County, Florida (NMSP-06-08)

Olympic Coast National Marine Sanctuary Habitat Mapping: Survey report and classification of side scan sonar data from surveys HMPR-114-2004-02 and HMPR-116-2005-01 (NMSP-06-07)

A Pilot Study of Hogfish (*Lachnolaimus maximus* Walbaum 1792) Movement in the Conch Reef Research Only Area (Northern Florida Keys) (NMSP-06-06)

Comments on Hydrographic and Topographic LIDAR Acquisition and Merging with Multibeam Sounding Data Acquired in the Olympic Coast National Marine Sanctuary (ONMS-06-05)

Conservation Science in NOAA's National Marine Sanctuaries: Description and Recent Accomplishments (ONMS-06-04)

Normalization and characterization of multibeam backscatter: Koitlah Point to Point of the Arches, Olympic Coast National Marine Sanctuary - Survey HMPR-115-2004-03 (ONMS-06-03)

Developing Alternatives for Optimal Representation of Seafloor Habitats and Associated Communities in Stellwagen Bank National Marine Sanctuary (ONMS-06-02)

Benthic Habitat Mapping in the Olympic Coast National Marine Sanctuary (ONMS-06-01)

Channel Islands Deep Water Monitoring Plan Development Workshop Report (ONMS-05-05)

Movement of yellowtail snapper (Ocyurus chrysurus Block 1790) and black grouper (Mycteroperca bonaci Poey 1860) in the northern Florida Keys National Marine Sanctuary as determined by acoustic telemetry (MSD-05-4)

The Impacts of Coastal Protection Structures in California's Monterey Bay National Marine Sanctuary (MSD-05-3)

An annotated bibliography of diet studies of fish of the southeast United States and Gray's Reef National Marine Sanctuary (MSD-05-2)

Noise Levels and Sources in the Stellwagen Bank National Marine Sanctuary and the St. Lawrence River Estuary (MSD-05-1)

Biogeographic Analysis of the Tortugas Ecological Reserve (MSD-04-1)

A Review of the Ecological Effectiveness of Subtidal Marine Reserves in Central California (MSD-04-2, MSD-04-3)

Pre-Construction Coral Survey of the M/V Wellwood Grounding Site (MSD-03-1)

Olympic Coast National Marine Sanctuary: Proceedings of the 1998 Research Workshop, Seattle, Washington (MSD-01-04)

Workshop on Marine Mammal Research & Monitoring in the National Marine Sanctuaries (MSD-01-03)

A Review of Marine Zones in the Monterey Bay National Marine Sanctuary (MSD-01-2)

Distribution and Sighting Frequency of Reef Fishes in the Florida Keys National Marine Sanctuary (MSD-01-1)

Flower Garden Banks National Marine Sanctuary: A Rapid Assessment of Coral, Fish, and Algae Using the AGRRA Protocol (MSD-00-3)

The Economic Contribution of Whalewatching to Regional Economies: Perspectives From Two National Marine Sanctuaries (MSD-00-2)

Olympic Coast National Marine Sanctuary Area to be Avoided Education and Monitoring Program (MSD-00-1)

Multi-species and Multi-interest Management: an Ecosystem Approach to Market Squid (*Loligo opalescens*) Harvest in California (MSD-99-1)